Best Seller
is
Only the Beginning

By #1 International Best Selling Author
Steve Kidd

Copyright © 2022 Steve Kidd. All rights reserved. No part of this book can be reproduced in any form without the written permission of the author and its publisher

Table of Contents

Introduction 9

What Does Being a Best Seller Mean For You? 15

The Credential You Need 21

It's Just the Beginning! 37

Introduction

As I set out to write this book, my first thought was "what do people need and who even cares about being a bestseller?" Then I realized that any confusion around what a bestseller is, where it fits in your marketing plan and why you need it, is because no one has taken the time to show you what being a bestseller means to YOU today!

Let me give you the perfect example of what a bestseller can do for you:

My good friend Carl Michel came to me with his finished book "365 Hip Hop." It is an amazing book. I really believe every person can benefit from his book, but especially parents of teens into hip-hop, or teens and young adults that listen to hip hop. This audience really needs to find the seeds of greatness in life - the ones that exist in some of the most unlikely of spots.

His gift was being able to take very popular songs - ones that would often be considered by parents to be demeaning and even destructive, and find points of true inspiration, motivation and transformation.

Carl is like a treasure-hunter, finding gold in songs that appeared void of redeeming qualities; being able to offer readers powerful messages out of seemingly worthless lyrics is such a gift.

But Carl had two problems: people did not understand how powerful, life-changing and necessary his message was, and he did not (yet) have the credentials to speak to his ideal audience.

Carl was on a mission to spread his message of hope, purpose and growth to high school age kids. He even offered to do it for free, but no one knew about his 'magic' and the life-changing outcomes from it. His calls were not returned.

You see, Carl lacked one thing: it wasn't drive; it wasn't ambition; nor it a lack of talent. He simply lacked the credential that certified what he did was something people should pay attention to. What Carl needed was something that set him apart. He needed that 'something' that people would immediately know he had the skills they needed.

He needed to be a best-seller!

That was when Carl came into my life and we made him a number one international best-selling author. I love how he puts it: *I can no longer be introduced as Carl Michel, I am international best-selling author, Carl Michel.*

That one credential made all the difference. That simple yet powerful title gave him instant authority. Because *Best-Selling Author* is the #1 influencer credential a person can currently have, it gives Carl, or anyone else who achieves this certification, the most powerful tool available: the one that expands influence. He used this title to further engineer his celebrity, respect and authority which ultimately allowed him to help more kids, and bring his vision to life. Carl went from people not returning his phone calls to speak for free, to being booked-out four to six months in advance at $2000 per speaking gig. He has gone on to be at the White House, on MTV a couple of times, along with doing many, many other celebrity, and public, appearances. He collects pictures of himself with the very artists whose songs he found motivations out of.

What Does Being a Best Seller Mean For You?

As you can see by Carl's story, becoming an Amazon bestseller was just the beginning!

The Amazon bestseller list is, of all the lists right now, the most accurate reflection of which books are the truly best-selling books currently. Whether your book is a bestseller for an hour, or like Carl Michel's, a top 10 on the bestseller list for more than six consecutive years now, the credential that matters is yours: a best-selling author!

Making people best-selling authors is what I do. I have done it 1000s of times now and the system I created is used around the world as the standard for becoming an Amazon bestseller. In fact it works so well I guarantee it! But that was just the foundation. Achieving bestseller status was only the beginning. Carl had to take that credential and use it for all the advantages it afforded him. I can say without reservation Carl has done an amazing job of continuing from that foundation I built for him as the starting point for his marketing. This author is continually doing the ongoing work, doing what he loves to do, building all of the powerful things he does on this platform. I built the foundation, he built the 'walls' and the 'roof,' if you will.

Interesting to Note:

Throughout all of history the capturing

and collection of words and ideas has always been an intricate part of who we are as people.

Long before the invention of the printing press, people were chiseling, drawing, creating thoughts, impressions and even abstract ideas into something more tangible. They wanted content that would outlast them.

When the printing press originally came into existence it was meant only for the preservation of the most sacred of texts. Now, it has grown to the point where printing is used for even the most mundane of doodles. This 'capturing and printing' does not by itself necessarily legitimize, or delegitimize, the words printed on the paper; they are simply expressions of the person who put their concepts down as written words. Whether it is a phone number or volume of encyclopedias, the 'capturing and printing' of information is important and necessary. It matters not if you are the next great literary master, or are simply capturing concepts from your own life and imaginations - all have value to the reader / recipient. Your message to the person you are meant to serve is water to a person lost in the desert.

Who you are and what you write is so needed, so valuable. The message you share is the beginning of the process of being who you were created to be in this world.

I already know that your book is necessary, powerful and most of all, it is needed. The legitimacy of bestseller validation speaks volumes to those you wish to serve, as well. It gets their attention. In fact, all of your future marketing must be based on the foundation, *bestseller,* in order to reach its maximum potential.

Becoming a bestseller is intentionally choosing to start that journey in an impactful and powerful way: with the number one tool of influence. Some people think becoming a best-selling author is the end game, but it is truly the beginning.

The Credential You Need

You are the expert of your story and the guru of who you are today; of what you have learned in life thus far. Your book is you telling the world what you have learned so far. Just like a medical degree, your best-selling book is verification that you can effectively repeat all that you have learned so far. It is the beginning achievement of your success.

We need to really look at becoming a best-selling author as your equivalent of graduating medical school and being certified with the credential of doctor. The certification of your title as a doctor when you graduate medical school is just the beginning...

There is a strong parallel between a best-selling author and becoming a medical doctor. We all have seen the concepts on TV and have a general understanding of a doctor's journey. To become a medical doctor you go to school for a very long time. And when you graduate medical school you are legally and officially Dr. You. You have the legal right, for the rest of your life, to put "Dr." in front of your name or "MD" behind your name. The title is a reflection of you having proven your knowledge mastery and have completed a recognized credentialing program. You are certified as MD, or PhD, or JD (Juris Doctorate - law degree.)

So, you graduate medical school and you are now Dr. So-and-So. As you walk across the stage they give you your certificate that says "Congratulations!" Well, I mean it actually says that you graduated, but you know the short version is that it says 'congratulations, you are officially an indebted medical doctor.'

Now that doesn't mean you can go out, grab a prescription pad, start prescribing medicine to people or open up a doctor's office. In order to be board certified, you learn while working as an intern under trained doctors. You learn how to actually put into practice the things you learned in books, labs, on mannequins and cadavers.

Working as an intern, you get a supervised opportunity to work on an actual human being. The downside of being an intern is that you work the worst shifts, with the worst of all duties to carry-out, as the lowest level of personnel. You learn, learn, learn, learn and eventually your internship is over.

But what does that mean? It's easier to say what it doesn't mean: you still don't get to use that prescription pad or have a grand opening for your office. Oh, no, no...now you get to go through residency. At least now you don't have somebody looking over your shoulder, breathing down your neck saying "you did it wrong" every time. At least now you're given a little bit of leeway, a little bit of opportunity to *show* what you know versus tell what you know.

Practice drills and rehearsal of skills continue until you reach a demonstrable level of proficiency to be a full blown doctor.

There is some light at the end of that tunnel: following residency you are now considered a "GP." This could be a general practice doctor, a general surgeon or a GP in whichever is your field of choice.

If you want to specialize, be it as a psychiatrist or a brain surgeon, you go through more training, a fellowship, more specialized training. All this just so you can wield a prescription pad, do surgery, or prescribe medication to your psychiatry patients.

And then you would think after all of that now, you could rest on your laurels and do that thing that you were born to be and show it to a whole world. But in truth, even then, you the doctor will be required, *for the rest of your life,* to take a certain number of hours of continuing education every year in order to remain certified both in your specialized field as well, generally, in the field of medicine.

Just like a doctor keeps learning and growing, you, too, will continue to learn and then apply, learn some more, make mistakes, adjust, learn, grow, and change. That's what professional development, and life, is all about: never-ending growth lending itself toward your personal 'advanced degree' in what you know best.

You are an expert right now!
The world needs you right now!

Just as the launch of "365 Hip Hop" was the start for all that Carl Michel has done, is doing and will do in the world, just as his becoming International best-selling Author was only the beginning so too you need this beginning. You need to build on it and from it in order to have the credentialing you need and deserve as well as the firm foundation that allows maximum potential and accelerated results and reach.

The reason why I go into the extreme detail of that is because that's a perfect example of the difference between what we often think of when we think of a bestseller, and the reality of what it *really* is.

The reality of being a doctor doesn't happen on grad night yet that credential is needed to start that journey. It is the same idea with being a credentialed bestseller: it opens those doors for you just like it did for Carl.

When we helped Dr. Draion Burch create his book, done with one purpose in mind: his course. That course, based on his international bestseller, generated more than $160,000 in the first 60 days. His bestseller was just the beginning of results such as those.

Let's say you did the same, offering a $1,000 course, and your goal was $100k. Only 100 courses versus *how* many books you would need to sell? There is no comparison.

I've been selling since I was five years old. That's 50 years. I can tell you that one of the hardest sales tasks you could ever possibly take on, if you want to make substantial money, would be selling books one at a time. Making hundreds of thousands of dollars, $2 or $3 at a time off Amazon sales, is a very long, hard grind. Compare that to creating a course based on your best-selling book. When it comes to sales and building a successful business that generates serious revenue, a course based on a bestseller is one of the most impactful things you can sell.

When you tell somebody you're a best-selling author they trust and believe in you, too. I mean, what a powerful piece of clout it is to say 'I wrote the best-selling book on that.' You wrote the book, you got in the door, you earned the right by telling them what you know; to be able to show them what you told them; to be able to do for them what you said you could.

Just one more time: becoming a best-selling author is only the beginning.

Certification from an outside source, (in this case, Amazon, the place that sells most of the books in the world) makes a huge difference in perception, too. It truly does grab your audience's attention. It is a stamp on your life that validates what is already true.

Now you've achieved this certification, because you're legitimately ranked on Amazon, whether it be for an hour, or maybe even it's ranked for years, you've told the world this is your time: that you've earned the right to use the title, *because you have.*

You have put in the hours, have the experience, and continue to learn. You never stop getting more and more and becoming better and better at it over and over again until you truly are the guru that you always were inside.

There is no one like you! You are the expert at being you and doing what you do, being who you are. You know that success is not a destination but a journey. In fact, you wrote the book on it.

When we come to the end of our life; when we break the tape and we are the winner of the race that was our life (which you will be), you get to choose how big of a victory it is! Right now, the race of your life is so far from over. There is so much more learning and growing and developing to go. Becoming a bestseller is just the beginning. It is where you truly start to play full-out and make your life win a big one.

Get the attention of the person you are meant to serve!

Tell them you have what they are looking for!

Earn the right to show them just how much you can change their life!

It's ironic, but often in the business industry we skip the step of credentialing ourselves first. Credentialing is simply *telling* the person what we know in order to earn the right to be able to then *show* the person what we know.

There is nothing like the power of a third party saying something is of note, or if you will, a "certification" of who we are.

As a marketing expert for more than 30 years I know that "bestseller" is THE credential needed for maximum certification and marketing effectiveness. It is the foundation; the starting point to all that we will do; all that our marketing will say about us.

Again, just like the diplomas at each level, this, too, is the certification from the source (Amazon) that you passed the test and got the credential that speaks volumes to your audience. It is 'telling' and you get to 'show' how you are the master of what you know. Of course you are. You will always be the greatest expert in what you know, in BEING YOU and in sharing all that you hold to be true! After you become a best-selling author, you are going to get book reviews and client testimonials from people that you've worked with that are going to say things about you and your genius. Indeed, those are going to be further validation. You just have to start from the credential process to gain maximum effectiveness for all your hard work. You have to start from knowing what you know and being able to tell the world what you know. You need to share what you're an expert at and how they will benefit from the wisdom you've come to share. It begins with acknowledged credentialing of your brilliance.

When you saw on the cover that this is my 20th number one international best-selling book, did it spark your attention? I'll go so far as to say that you may have found this subconsciously working on you when you chose to get this book. The credential makes a difference.

I love writing books, and I love making authors bestsellers. This is less about ego boosting (well, OK, some of it is); it is more about getting your attention. I have a point I want to make: I want to earn the right to be able to help *you* make the difference you've come to make in this world. In order to do that I've got to be the first one to practice what I preach: not just make myself a bestseller, or tell you that I've been a bestseller, but *show* you by doing it again and again.

I can tell you client testimonials and experiential testimonials of people that

I've worked with, but the point is that I earned the right by simply having the shingle out in front that says *I'm a best-selling author, first.*

It's Just the Beginning!

Becoming a bestseller is just the beginning, the foundational piece that all of your marketing is going to be based upon, whether it's a giveaway or a $100k program, matters not. When someone visits your site and you offer "10 Tips based on my international best-selling book" you've got their attention. It's a stand out over the typical opt-in page everyone has these days. That visitor is going to be further enrolled in testing the waters with you than if you simply had "10 Tips" offered. I know, some things are obvious.

It all starts at the top of your website where your name is highlighted: *international best-selling author.*

When you appear on podcasts, your introduction will begin with *international best-selling author: International best-selling author, Steve Kidd is here today to show you how to reach the goals you've always dreamed of, and how to help the people that you were born to serve.*

Oh that's good marketing language isn't it?

You want to know more about that topic, don't you?

From this point, you build the relationship gained from your credential. Even if you are a first time author, you have gained credibility from a globally-recognized leader. This is third party validation from a giant: Amazon accounts for over 90% of all book sales, worldwide.

Imagine the impact of offering your course, *"based on my international best-selling book."* Again, good marketing language. And that's what this is really about: positioning you in the best light, in the best ways available, to do the work you've been born to do.

I mention this is my personal 20th best-selling book, but it is also one of the literally 1000s of books I have helped people write, publish and market to bestseller status. My signature system guides you in succinctly speaking your truth, your story; then facilitates your words into a powerfully written book. This system has also been taught to many people. Just about anyone you meet offering a "become a bestseller" program, (whether they know this or not), is probably using my system. Heck, I have done this so long I have even been sales-pitched by other people on bestseller programs that use my signature system!

I have been in marketing all my life, it seems. As mentioned earlier, I started selling at age five, was a sales manager and trainer by age 19, and then started my marketing company in 1988. During that time, I have worked with so many amazing people, ranging from startups to multi-billionaires. I even consulted with the Coca-Cola Company when their Vitamin Water division became the official sponsor of the 3rd movie in the *Twilight* saga, *Eclipse*. What a great story that is...

I've been doing books since 2007 when I first edited, formatted and published a book tracking the steps of this epic film series. The book was based on the travels and locations for the filming of the original *Twilight* movie. These had been chronicled by my former wife and second youngest child, all from a unique perspective. In fact, the book was written based on their mother-daughter trip for my daughter's 18th birthday.

They were on a mission to find all the designated book locations in Forks, WA, as well as all the filming locations for the original *Twilight* movie, filmed in and around Portland, OR.

This book was wildly popular. To this day, I still get calls from people about it.

Well, to be honest, that comes as a result of the marketing we did for the book. Generating a following that picks up the phone, to this day, is remarkable, not impossible. You see, at the time, our book was the best-selling movie travel guide on Amazon. And it led to so many things, not the least of which included being recognized by Coca-Cola. *They* reached out to *me* for help, support and advice on how to best reach the fan base of raving *Twilight* fans. Making this book a bestseller was just the beginning: there were more ways, (and things), I got to market to this fan base after making that movie travel guide a best-selling book.

Writing, publishing and marketing books to bestseller status rose from the humble beginning and success of that one book. It parlayed into being all that my marketing company does: work with authors. Because - That's right, say it with me :) - *Bestseller is Only the Beginning.*

I love marketing! I love books! But mostly, it is my great honor to help share amazing people just like you with the world.

Is your vision big? How about *'is it big enough?'* What starts out right ends up right. Your bestseller can lead you and those you serve to the next level. In fact, with the right marketing plan in play, it isn't a long reach to imagine this being true for you: *"...come join the course based on my international best-selling book that thousands upon thousands of people have now read."*

Or, *"based on my best-selling book, this course has helped hundreds of people change their lives."*

Just getting started with your bestseller? How does *"Amazon lists this book as a #1 international bestseller in 5 categories across 4 different countries,"* sound to you? How strong of an opening is that?

Begin by sharing who you are today; what you know right now. My eight year old granddaughter wrote a book about meeting the best of best friends in the whole wide world. It's what she knew and shared. It is an amazing and insightful little story that helps people learn the child-like art of friendship and how to celebrate it.

Maybe your book is about overcoming the struggles or the traumas you have gone through; or, it could be a simple task you're good at: the *one* thing you know really well, right now. For instance, are you one of those people who has no problem keeping up the dishes, or "doing the dishes"? In your mind you think, 'that's no big deal, everybody knows how to do dishes.' Consider this: there is somebody out there, right now, trying to "do the dishes." For some reason, it's something they struggle with every day. Naturally, they fight against it.

It's always surprising to me because I've been doing dishes pretty much my whole life, but there are people who really do not know how to hand wash a dish. There are many people who don't even know how to properly load a dishwasher. They fill the machine, but the dishes come out as dirty, or dirtier, than they went in.

Now, you may be thinking to yourself, *but that's so easy*. It is to you, but for them that struggle is real every single day. Imagine the difference you can make just sharing your top five tricks to getting those dishes done.

Here's a thought: for those struggling, perhaps it isn't the process of simply cleaning the dishes, it's the trauma behind it. You know, maybe it's a person whose parents were a little bit abusive and doing the dishes is a recurring, minor post traumatic event for them. As you can imagine, if they were mentally or physically abused, "doing dishes" triggers them every time. And maybe you went through that, too. However, you've learned how to be able to turn something as simple as "doing dishes" do-able...fun, even. You share about how you learned to turn doing these 'triggering dishes' into the best time of your day: one where you put on headphones and listen to a series of songs that refresh your soul.

Let's say you go further, telling them about this special dish soap that lifts you up. You bought it because it refreshes your soul. Suddenly, "doing dishes" becomes a five minute, or a 20 minute, solace period each day. You are showing them how you transitioned from something that triggered you emotionally to what is now the best part of the day. What was once a trauma is now the thing they look forward to every day. Don't discount that simple thing that you do so easily! It might literally be what others need in their lives. Until you share what you know, they are stuck on a 'spin cycle.'

Think of the 'work' you have been doing without being paid for it. Your wisdom, captured in a best-selling book, gives you the attention and recognition you deserve in a way that reaches those who need your know-how. Building a business, answering your calling, expressing your soul's purpose…all of it starts with you obtaining the most widely accepted #1 influencer credential there is currently: *best-selling author*. There is value in your experience and your book positions you with authority, credibility and expertise. Obtaining your best-selling author credential is how you reach the next level with what you know best.

> *"I have gotten more credibility and more exposure from being a best-selling author than I have from being a doctor in my field for more than 20 years."*
> **Dr. Alisha Griffith**, client

Growth never stops. You will continue to be an ever-expanding version of yourself: you, the expert at what you know. There is no one else who can do what you do; no one else who puts it quite 'that way' like you do.

Imagining that you will be reaching people in a whole new way isn't imaginary, then, is it? It is a reality. It is a fact.

Best-Selling Author is simply a validation from an outside source you can use to your advantage because it is, in part, what other people look for; how you get their attention.

Bestseller status is not the be-all, end-all…oh, no, no, it is just the beginning. It's that graduation moment every med school student has en route to his goal of serving the health care needs of others. His journey, and yours, starts with that credential. You gain the benefit of the ranking, "bestseller" again for a day, a week, a month or a 10 years.

One word of caution: please don't buy into the hype that you will eventually become a best-seller. It might happen, but decades of experience in online marketing and publishing have shown me otherwise: it takes a system, and wisdom behind that system, to deliver on the promise literally thousands of authors have already benefited from using. I created that system.

If you don't consider yourself a writer, don't fret. In my book, "**Become a bestseller Today: How to and why you need to be a bestseller**," there are alternative methods designed for your book to 'come out' of you very quickly.

I really love helping people discover how to put their book out now...jump the line...because doing it quickly, easily and effectively is available to you, today.

Hopefully, after reading this, you want to be a bestseller. It is the solid core and foundation for the beginning of your journey, and the building of your platform.

I invite you to talk in more detail. Let's discuss how you can become a bestseller on a free call with me. Let's talk about where you are and what you need. In this complementary first call, I want to help you as much as possible for the time we have together. If there is more that I can help you with from there, we can do that.

Go to:

bestsellerisonlythebeginning.com

I look forward to talking with you and celebrating all of your successes. I am here for you, already cheering you on.

You are going to change the world simply by sharing who you are. It is "enough" and much-needed. With that light of yours shining, you become a catalyst for change. It's no wonder I love my job: because I've helped thousands of people just like you.

I can't wait to speak with you, *Future International Best-Selling Author, YOU.*
As you know, *a best-seller* is only the beginning! Let's see where this can take *you*, next.

www.ingramcontent.com/pod-product-compliance
Lightning Source LLC
Chambersburg PA
CBHW050302220526
45465CB00002B/790